SUBWAY LIFE

An Underground Guide to Balanced Living

JEFF PASQUALE

Editor: Kammy Wood

Cover Concept: Kammy Wood and Vanessa Nicole Ortiz

Text layout and design: Fagaras Codrut Sebastian

∼

For my father, Anthony Victor Pasquale
who taught me, by example,
the values of authenticity, simplicity,
and consistency.

∼

Contents

Introduction vii

I.   Circumstances and Decisions 1
     1.   Finding the Right Entrance 3
     2.   (Almost) Everyone Pays 9
     3.   Expect Lines 13

II. Navigating Through Life 17
     4.   Choosing the Right Train 19
     5.   Be Ready for Competition
          (Even on the Subway) 25
     6.   Finding a Seat 31
     7.   Expect to Get Bounced Around 35

III. Relating 39
     8.   Greeting and Connecting With Other People 41
     9.   Sharing 47
     10. Saying "Please" and "Thank You" 51
     11. Giving 55

IV. Responding 59
     12. Being Aware of Fellow Travelers 61
     13. You May Be Annoyed By Others 65
     14. Transfers Are Normal (So is Change) 69

V.   Awareness and Intention 73
     15. Getting Off at the Right Stop 75
     16. Knowing What Time It Is 79
     17. Emerge Smiling 83

The End of the Ride Is Just The Beginning 85

Assessment and Review 91

Acknowledgements 103

L ife is often like a subway ride. Actually, it's more like riding the subway without holding on.

In life, as on the subway, you can expect a jolt at the beginning and at the end of the ride—along with all of those bumps, shakes, and shudders that will knock you down if you're not holding on.

And don't forget the sudden darkness that occurs from time to time, which can add to your confusion.

In life, there is no right or wrong path; it's different for everybody. Only you can know what is right for you.

This is a reference book that intends to offer insight and perspective. Each chapter has a different focus, which uses the analogy of the subway to illustrate the unique aspects of the experience we call life.

The subway in New York City has undergone some radical changes since its dark days in the 1970s. Back then, the subway was a scary place where passengers rarely looked at each other, much less acknowledged each other's presence. The standard mandate that parents gave to their children applied to adults as well: "Don't talk to strangers."

But today, the subway is very different. There is a renewed sense of connectedness, a feeling that people really are in this together. Passengers now regularly make eye contact, give nods of hello, and even engage in conversation. The subway has been transformed into a cleaner, safer, and more pleasant environment with millions of people flowing through it day and night. The New York City subway is once again a truly amazing experience.

Just how is life like the subway?

There are times when we are racing to catch a train, literally. But more often, it's a metaphor. We feel like we've missed the train, or worse, we feel we're on the wrong train. These are all analogies for how we live our lives today. We race from one task to another, getting bumped around in the process, thus missing out on a lot of essential experiences in our daily lives.

Our values and behaviors are based on what we've observed, but we often miss the subtle meaning of the simplest gestures, such as a smile or an offered seat, because of the noise of life that's going on around us.

While comparing life to a subway ride might seem a bit silly, when you consider the variety of people and circumstances in the world today, and the array of people who come together on the subway, it makes sense.

The subway is simply a microcosm of life—every day, the rhythm and diversity of all humanity is there on display: joy and sadness, struggle and triumph, introverts trying to hide in their books, extroverts striking up a conversation with the strangers sitting beside them. It's all there to observe and participate in ... in life and on the subway.

Trains and people are everywhere, and people are people no matter where we go— New York, London, Sydney, Hong Kong, or Wichita. So consider Subway Life as a representation of the events in your life. It's a way to live and deal with other people—at home, on the street, or below it.

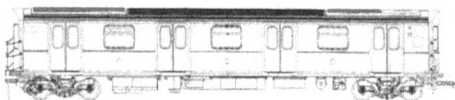

An Underground Guide to Balanced Living

I CIRCUMSTANCES AND DECISIONS

A friend of mine once traveled to New York City to attend a meeting for his company. He ventured into the subway to go from midtown to the upper west side. He didn't realize that he had entered a transfer station where many subway lines converged, enabling commuters to easily change trains.

Underground, the signs pointed in every direction. People rushed past him as though the station was on fire. He felt as though he might drown in the concussive noise of trains, horns, rushing feet, and the endless sea of competing conversations. He wanted to stop someone and ask where he was and where he should go. But how? Would that person even hear him?

He decided to study a subway map on the wall. He made his choice, and jumped on a train. But that train was the wrong one. So he doubled back to the original station, eyeing his watch, and anxiously stopped a man, hoping for directions. "Take the A train going uptown. It's an express," the stranger informed him, and sped off into the shifting crowd.

Now my lost friend knew which train to take, but not which side of the platform he ought to be on.

Another train came along; he thought it said A on the front, so he boarded it. It was the right train but—again—it was going in the wrong direction.

Now he was really late. He doubled back, again, for one more attempt. Another train had just arrived. After a deep breath, he asked the conductor if that was the right train. "No," the conductor told him. "The train you need is on the other side of these tracks," he said, motioning to the other side.

My friend took another deep breath and exhaled. Up the stairs, across, and back down again. Finally, the right train.

My friend took a cab back to his hotel that night.

Some people consider life one continuous adventure—for them, having a specific destination isn't imperative, so any entrance will do.

But most of us want to get somewhere, and we'd like to get there as quickly and efficiently as possible.

Finding the right subway entrance can be much like finding the right house to live in, the right car to drive, the right doctor to see, the right college to attend, or the right job. There may be an abundance of information before you, or you may find there is none. In tense, time-sensitive situations, your best choice is to process and prioritize whatever information is in front of you and make your decision.

Despite our intentions to do otherwise, we all go through life taking missteps, going through wrong doors, making wrong turns, and generally stepping into crap, yet we all survive to live another day.

99.9% of us find the right entrance—the right door, the right job, the right partner, the right life choices—maybe not always the first time, but we eventually figure it out. So if you're about to make a big life decision, get a good map or good instructions. Don't be afraid to ask for directions (guys), and double-check the signs before you walk through the entrance.

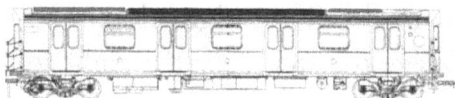

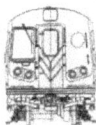

An unfortunate reality about the New York City subway system today is that with the high cost of a ticket, more and more people are opting to risk a $100 fine rather than paying the $2.50 ticket price or the $29 weekly MetroCard fee.

A 2009 study estimated that fare-beaters did not pay 18.5 million times (or 50,684 times a day) that year, and the number of people caught was only 120,000.

What does that say about the integrity of subway riders? What does that say about the price of a subway ticket? And what does that say about a city's ability to enforce its laws?

Do not get caught up in the philosophical implications of the above questions. **What really matters here is: what would you do when presented with the opportunity to cheat the system?** Your answer reveals your level of integrity and how you are wired.

People jump the turnstile or cheat in life for as many reasons as there are people. Sometimes it is out of need, but many times people do it because they've justified it in some way. Your decisions, good and bad, affect how you feel about yourself and ultimately how you relate and connect to other people.

The reality in life is that if you cheat (steal a newspaper, drive over the speed limit, or fudge on your taxes), the likelihood of getting caught is slim. Meaning the only thing stopping you is that very thin line called your personal standards, also known as your integrity.

Cultural and personal standards collapse when a large portion of the population begins following the standard of what is good for them as individuals versus what's good for the group. I'm not talking about socialism. I'm talking about when a parent chooses to break the law, gets arrested and his/her family suffers. Or when a leader of a company gets caught with his hands in the till and the company falters and people lose their jobs. Or when a political leader chooses to cheat on his wife and is found out, he harms his family and the people he serves, often on a large scale.

In other words: **paying your share is a personal choice.**

It's a personal standard and a moral one. It represents fairness, accountability, and reciprocity. It means that you pay (or work) for something because you want to, not because you have to.

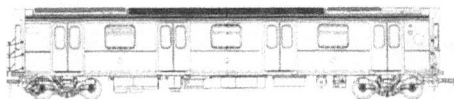

Whether you're buying a MetroCard, waiting for a train, or waiting to get off a train, you're going to wait in lines. Life works the same way.

A line represents a delay, and delays typically prevent us from doing that next important thing we want to do. For some people, the next thing may be nothing more than watching TV or taking a nap. Lines and delays often draw out and exacerbate the self-importance in all of us.

The aversion to lines is burned into the American psyche. It doesn't matter where the line is, it simply must be avoided at all costs. Once, I watched a driver cross five lanes of traffic on the interstate doing 70 MPH during rush hour to avoid a line. (Yes, it can be done.) I've also witnessed a family of five split up and steer themselves into separate lines at Target in order to supposedly get out of the store more quickly.

Not all people are in such a glorious hurry. There are patient people who are saints. They will accept practically anything that happens to them with serenity and a smile. The event was cancelled after waiting in line for an hour? No problem. The store is closing and she has to come back tomorrow? Not a problem. A man is quietly humming to himself and ten people have just cut in front of him—*No problem*, he thinks, and keeps humming. After all, those people probably have somewhere they need to be.

There is one other group of waiters-in-line. I'll call them the extremists. They are small in number, but they are in such a tremendous hurry that they either leave in a huff, or decide they are important enough to sidle their way to a better spot in the line (with a look of feigned innocence). How you respond to them, or not, is up to you.

All we can do with lines is respond to them.

We can't make them faster or shorter but we can choose to accept that lines will always exist.

The reality is that life, and the subway, is full of people of all shapes, sizes, and attitudes, and many times they will all be in line ahead of you.

So if you're not a fan of crowds, and you're not good with lines, the subway may be a challenge for you.

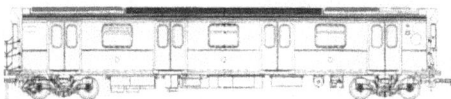

II NAVIGATING THROUGH LIFE

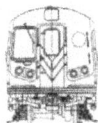

Decisions, decisions. What can you do? This time, you've chosen the right entrance and you know where you need to go, but you're in a hurry, you're running late, and you're not sure which train to take to save time. Is it the F, the M, the 2, or the 3?

Life is exactly like this. You suddenly feel as though you're surrounded by a multitude of options and there is precious little time to decide. Welcome to the real world.

Not true!

In this case, life is very different from a subway ride.

We all experience deadline pressure differently, especially when we're faced with a big decision. Most of this pressure comes from fear of looking like a fool, and we create an internal drama about how disastrous our decision will be if we're wrong.

The noise of life can create confusion, too. And when you're trying to make an important personal decision, the more choices you have in front of you, the more you may feel as though you're being tugged in many different directions.

Having choices is always a good thing. (Not everyone will agree.)

Some folks would rather choose between only chocolate and vanilla. But choices give us opportunities. They make us think and they allow us to grow.

The key to making better choices for ourselves is knowing *what we want* and *how to tune out the outside noise* that's trying to influence us (pressure from friends and family, advertisements, product placement, testimonials, etc.) Our families and friends usually want what's best for us, but they may approach the issue from *their own* perspective.

Companies produce a different kind of noise and have very different goals. They pay billions of dollars every year to influence our decisions because they know advertising works. They want us to choose them.

So it's up to us to learn how to discern when we're being advised and when we're being influenced (for better or worse). We need to know, with some degree of certainty, that we are reading the signs (or interpreting the ads) correctly. When we can see the difference, we will know that our decision truly is *our* decision.

It's important to remember that very few life decisions will require you to be exact, or require that you make a choice on the spot. So relax, take your time, think through your plans. Carefully consider your options, then choose wisely. Remember, when it comes to choices, life is not always like the subway. (Thank God.)

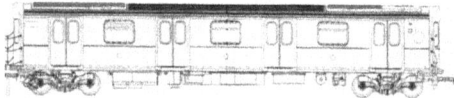

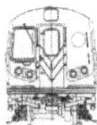

If you've ever been on a subway platform at rush hour waiting for a train, you know that people can be competitive, if not downright rude and aggressive.

In life you come up against similar motivations in people. Instead of jockeying for entry onto the next train, they're positioning themselves for the next opportunity to make money, get a promotion, receive a bonus, or purchase a limited-supply toy or gadget that's gone on sale.

Billy Joel used to end his notoriously long concert performances by saying, "Don't take any shit from anybody," offering a blunt reminder that not everyone out there has your best interest at heart. So remember, as you stand at the entrance of a subway door amidst a sea of fellow travelers, who are all intent on getting on that train, to be prepared for a little tussle. There's no avoiding it on the subway.

None of us look forward to the daily battle with coworkers, neighbors, and fellow travelers.

The secret to avoiding a daily struggle is to disengage.

Don't buy into the concept that you always have to get the best parking spot or the fastest line in the store. Whether we participate in those competitive games or not, they will still go on without us.

It takes sharp awareness to recognize when someone is competing with us. Competition is not evil. It just *is*. In life, people compete to be first in line, or to get a good seat in a restaurant. Those situations happen every day. We all choose which games we want to play and how we'll compete in them. This choice comes from our view of life.

Is your life really going to be ruined if you don't get those tickets? Will your day be wrecked because you were 25th in line at the most popular deli in town?

None of this applies if you're competing for a job or an award that will have a big financial impact on your life. These are cases where you must be ready to compete if you intend to win that job or award. But if you come unglued because a limited supply of $500 fifty-inch plasmas sold out one person ahead of you, your life isn't over. It's just a television.

You don't have to live your life with a dog-eat-dog attitude. Just know that people will sometimes choose to be aggressive about things that are not very important to you. The challenge comes when there is something you do want, and the people around you want it just as badly.

How you respond in competitive situations reflects the kind of person you are. Are you a "scarcity-minded" individual? Or do you live with an *abundance mentality*? If you believe in abundance, you already know that you don't need to push your way onto the train—there will always be another one.

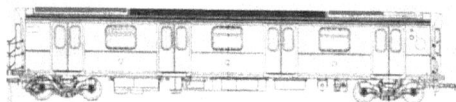

One of the biggest challenges of riding the subway is finding a seat. But a seat isn't always as coveted a prize as you may think. Those who ride the subway know that if you're in a seat on the subway during rush hour, chances are near one hundred percent that you'll spend most of your ride with a straphanger[1] hovering over you.

For a long subway ride, a good seat is an important part of your journey.

It's the same thing in life: find a spot, get comfortable, don't be too picky about where you're located, and enjoy the ride. Sometimes you'll get what you want. Sometimes not.

---

1   Straphanger – a passenger who stands and hangs on to the overhead handles of a subway car.

Many times it is not uncommon to see both men and women offering their seat to a child or to an older person. But in other situations the subway has a strange effect on people.

Just for fun, simply watch the game of musical chairs play out. The doors open and people shuffle in. The warning bell sounds, the doors begin to close, and on cue, grown adults start diving toward open seats.

One time, I witnessed a woman slide in ahead of a man who was halfway through the process of sitting down, and he ended up in her lap. Occasionally, words are exchanged; otherwise only angry or hurt looks are offered. To the swiftest go the spoils.

On the subway, the cars closest to the exits are usually the most crowded. But most people would rather not search for a less crowded car, so they congregate at the center and endure. You will rarely find a seat if you follow this strategy.

In life above ground, scenes like these happen all the time—in grocery store lines, in parking lots, and outside great restaurants.

Buying a house can be like this, too. Just like a plum subway seat during rush hour, the best-looking house may not always be as it appears. There may be hidden structural issues. You may have noisy neighbors. There might be an abandoned landfill two miles away that reminds you it's there when the wind blows from the east.

On the subway, despite the fierceness of the sport, once the crowd has settled into the subway cars and it's apparent there are no seats left, alert strangers begin to offer their seats to children and those in obvious need.

There are many tactics you can employ to find a good seat, but choose wisely—the best seat on the subway may actually contain a mysterious clear liquid spilled by a previous passenger, so always look down.

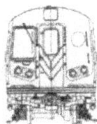

The subway may seem like an odd analogy for life. But life is much more like a subway ride than a clichéd roller coaster.

Life is about other people *and* you—how you respond to them, how they respond to you, how you respond to changes in your moods, and how you respond to those pleasant and not so pleasant situations that pop up. At the end of some days you will feel beaten up and used; other days, your journey may leave you feeling overwhelmed. But most days are uneventful, like subway rides, so it's best to make the most of the lack of drama.

You expect to get bounced around on the subway, so you hold on. Life is no different.

Bumps and bounces occur daily in our lives. Some are good, and some are not so good. If you do your best to anticipate the bumps, then you can take ease in the knowledge that you've done all you can. Expecting to get bumped or bounced around doesn't mean that you expect the worst from life; it just means that you are prepared to deal with problems as they come up. A bump in life might be a lost wallet or a newly discovered nick in your car bumper.

Like a subway ride, no one is immune to getting knocked around. If you've experienced a series of hard knocks in life, you know there's no guarantee that it won't happen again.

How you feel about getting bounced around is the way you view your life. Do you become unraveled if you get stuck at a railroad crossing for thirty minutes, or do you use that time to relax and listen to music? Do you see it as an opportunity to catch up on phone calls?

Will a flat tire ruin your day, or is it one of those frustrating things that happen occasionally?

Knowing that these things can and do happen, how do you typically respond to the bumps that occur in your life?

During a subway ride, you can observe the different ways people respond to the train's erratic motion. Some people will be surprised and bump into their neighbor, others will be firmly planted in their seat. Those on their feet may gently bend with the movement. A select few individuals will continue to do what they were doing—reading, sleeping, talking— undisturbed, as if the train were motionless.

Practicing anticipation is yet another choice we have. We can continue to repeat our same old reactive patterns or we can anticipate what will happen and just go with the flow. By anticipating, we become one with our environment and we can to stay focused on what we are doing. Learn to respond to your environment.

Live your life to the fullest, but be prepared for situations that may knock you off balance. Avoid living in fear of the bumps, jolts, and jerks (both the noun and the verb) in life. Focus on enjoying the ride instead of fearing it. If you prepare your response in advance, you will be much less surprised by life's sudden movements.

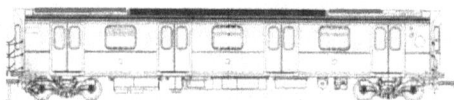

III | RELATING

Acknowledging the people around you can be an amazing way to grow as a person. It opens the door to conversation and for the sharing of thoughts and ideas. Given the rise in popularity of digital devices, it seems that most people would rather live their lives quietly and (mostly) undisturbed by the outside world as they go about their day.

It used to be that a subway ride meant walking straight into the car and finding a seat or a place to stand, while continuously looking down. Back then, eye contact was the kiss of death. If someone caught you looking at them, if only for a moment, you could easily have had some problems coming your way.

Most people riding the subway back then ignored one another and quietly hoped that trouble wouldn't find them. The only voice you heard on the subway in those times was the conductor announcing each station.

It's very different now, although many people still keep to themselves out of habit.

While it's true that we all need quiet time, it shouldn't be to the consistent exclusion of the outside world. We are not ants. We were not designed to exclusively sleep, eat, work, and relate to two or three people in our lives.

We are blessed with ears, eyes, and mouths for a reason. As social animals, we are not meant to live alone surrounded by thousands of other people. Much isolating behavior originates from fear – fear of being judged or made fun of—so some people avoid putting themselves in these situations by simply ignoring those around them. If we've learned this behavior from our parents, it will take some work to break down those walls.

Interestingly, some psychologists have suggested that our ability to smile and connect with strangers is also a reflection of our own level of happiness.

Life is going to be an adventure whether you live in a cave or a castle.

And dealing with other people is a necessity at many points in your life whether you like it or not. So why not choose to get used to it? Resolve to live adventurously and say *hello* to people. Watch what happens. See the doors open up … even on the subway.

Connecting with people affords incalculable possibilities simply because one person made the decision to say *hello*, in an attempt to connect with a stranger. New business opportunities, new relationships, and new partnerships all can be forged by the simple act of saying *hello*.

Make the effort to connect with others on a regular basis—not because a book told you to do it, but because you want to fully connect with the world around you.

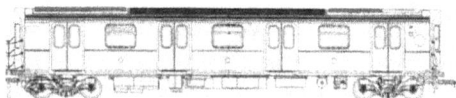

An Underground Guide to Balanced Living

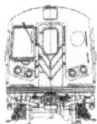

This might appear to be a lightweight topic for a subway ride, but it's serious. It's not about getting on the train with a pack of gum and sharing it with your neighbors, but it's close. You have many things you can share, even if you have no money in your pocket. Every day, you can share your smiles, your thoughts, a joke, or your newspaper, above ground or on the subway.

In life, sharing can wear many hats—you can share things (gum, tools, books), share power (as in authority or decision-making), share the spotlight (or, more practically, the focus of attention), or share the credit (by letting others be recognized for their efforts, too).

Each action (offering or receiving) is a conscious decision that most of us make.

The secret to a happier life is not just choosing to be happier, but choosing to share more frequently.

Sharing means not being attached to things or experiences.

Sharing should be automatic (without thought).

Sharing has its risks. People you share with can take it wrong way or feel that it's not enough. (In either case, it's their problem, not yours.)

Sharing is contagious. Model the behavior you wish to see in the world around you.

Sharing is not about you. It's about the other person, but is does reveal who you are as a person.

Have you ever tried sharing with someone who did not want what you were offering? The ideal response is to choose not become angry with the person who has rebuffed you. It's not personal, so don't make it that way.

The moral? Sharing must be unconditional. You offer to share not for thanks, praise, or recognition, but because you want to. Period.

Many times it's the simple things in life that people appreciate the most—like sharing. Yet, it's the simple things that are the hardest for us to get into the habit of doing.

Consider your morning commute. Do you share the road? Do you let other drivers pass in front of you? And then there is the even bigger challenge—do you let that other driver have that parking space that you could have easily captured?

The secret to learning how to share, and share masterfully, is to practice it … a lot.

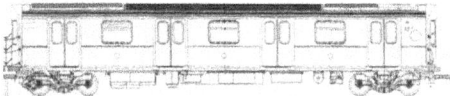

I once boarded a crowded subway car during rush hour along with a man in a disheveled business suit. He was struggling to keep his balance as he stood next to me. He wasn't drunk. He was completely exhausted. No seats were available for the long ride uptown, so he stood there with one hand on a hanger and the other one holding a briefcase.

Finally the crowd lightened, a seat became available, and he fell into it. At the next stop another large crowd boarded. A very pregnant woman searched for a seat with a hopeful look. But there were no seats available for her.

The exhausted man slowly stood up and motioned to the woman, and his empty seat.

"Please," he said.

"Thank you," she said with a grateful smile, and sat with an exhale of relief.

The man remained standing for the remainder of his trip.

There was no applause, no recognition, or nor were there any high-fives; it was a simple courtesy that took place in a sea of people. These acts are repeated many times every day.

The subway is probably the last place people would expect to hear the words *please* and *thank you*, but it's more common than you might think.

Unfortunately, in today's hurry-up society, it's sometimes easier to assume an attitude of busyness, where people may think—"I shouldn't have to say thank you; it's not that important."

The reality is that we live in a world where an expression of gratitude for a kindness offered is considered unnecessary, where it's considered okay to ask for help without any real sincerity. We say *please* and *thank you* because it's the civilized, courteous, and gracious thing to do...on the street or in the subway.

A genuine request for help (*Please?*)—and an offering of real thanks have great power.

When it comes to everyday kindnesses, offering a *please* or a *thank you* can have magical consequences. It will do you good to come out of your shell or your comfort zone and use these words more frequently and with feeling—even when you're on the subway.

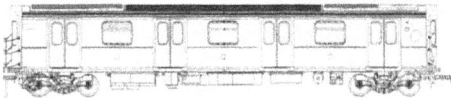

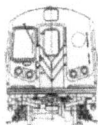

This is a trick title. Giving is really about love, and giving takes place every day in many forms—even on the subway.

Granted, when you get in a subway car you won't find the passengers engaged in a group hug, but you will see little acts of kindness—a woman giving up her seat to someone else, someone coming to the aid of another person who's fallen, a teenager helping someone who's lost, or a man listening to someone else's problem that he or she needs to share.

In most big cities (as on the subway), it's possible to cross paths with easily ten or more people each day who are looking for spare change from passersby. Personally, sometimes

I'm aware of them, and sometimes they become part of the landscape.

I once passed a man on the street in a wheelchair who was sitting erect, alert, and spoke clearly. A cluster of people, including myself, heard the man's appeal while shaking the coins in his paper coffee cup—"Any spare change?" he asked. All of us were on our way to somewhere else. And then, after a moment's pause—he said—"Please?!"

I stopped. He had finally gotten my attention. I circled back to the man and dropped some money into his cup. I had been pulled out of my dream. Sometimes, it takes a strong request in order to get our attention.

There are times when we justify to ourselves that we're just too busy to give, whether it's our time, money, or attention. If giving is important to you, whenever you catch yourself feeling too busy, ask yourself this simple question—"Where can I give back?" Pause for just a moment to let the question sink in, and then go back to what you were doing or thinking. An opportunity to give will always appear.

Giving someone your consideration, your time, your empathy, or your caring are all forms of love that you can give every day, everywhere you go.

Start your day intending to give, and end your day the same way. Notice how you feel. And recognize how the giving comes back to you—perhaps in the form of help getting off at the right stop.

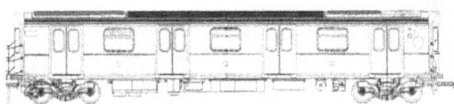

IV RESPONDING

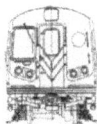

The subway isn't always the safest way to travel, but that doesn't stop over five million people from riding it each day. And the way people ensure their safety is by being aware of the people around them. No paranoia is necessary, just simple vigilance.

In life we all encounter people and circumstances that make us take pause. Our defenses are up, but we're not looking for battle; we're just prepared, aware. But staying aware isn't just for those times of possible danger; awareness is just as important when we're looking for opportunities—new jobs, new relationships, or new business offerings, for example.

Committing to awareness can be too big of a paradigm shift for some people to make, especially if they subscribe to the belief that life is always a half-empty glass. They choose to see the negative. For whatever reason, they have ended up seeing life (or a subway ride) as full of threats rather than opportunities. This viewpoint is almost always a choice.

Life is good. The idea is so popular that it has become a movie, a book, and a line of t-shirts. All of which were designed to make us more aware that there is a lot of good around us. But life certainly does have its bad elements. That's why being aware is so important.

There will be times when you will cross paths with people who look intimidating to you, and you may respond with hesitation. In reality they mean no harm; you've prejudged them, and you expect problems. The fact is anyone, no matter how we perceive them, has the ability to unpleasantly surprise us.

Your intuition and your life experiences are your greatest sources of security when dealing with other people.

The harsh words suddenly unleashed on you may be one person's response to having a bad day. Or those words could be a possible threat to you.

There's not enough time in life to analyze and hypothesize what that glance meant or what that gesture intended. In these situations, it's best to stay aware, take note, and move on.

Remember President Ronald Reagan's famous line while negotiating a nuclear arms treaty with the former Soviet Union: "Trust but verify." Be aware, trust your gut, and move on.

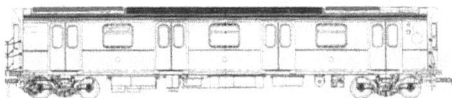

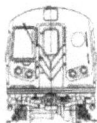

The subway has a unique and mysterious way of attracting the strangest individuals into its depths. (This is not to make fun or make light of people who are mentally disturbed. Truthfully, we all make judgments about others based on looks, behaviors, and smells.)

Sometimes in your life, you may feel you have those same magnetic powers. You may even find yourself asking, "Why do they always come to me?"

This is actually very funny. To hold yourself in such high or low esteem is really selfish. Catch yourself in the act and find a way to stop making everything all about you. Circumstances are what they are; some will be caused by you. Others not. That's all.

Sometimes the best way to deal with people who are bothering you is to smile at them and move on.

Years ago I worked in an office building that overlooked a busy intersection. Every day a tall African-American man stood on the corner for hours shouting at the traffic. As he shouted, he waved his arms violently. Everyone I knew who worked in the building avoided his corner of the intersection as they headed out for lunch. The man looked angry and menacing. Drivers and passersby were startled by his presence and made an effort to avoid entering his space.

One day I was returning to the office from my noontime run and was stopped by the traffic light. I turned and realized that the man had just joined me at the corner. He was easily seven feet tall. I looked up at him and he gave me a kind of a smirk, and jerked his head up in a nod as if he recognized me. Then he turned and began screaming at the traffic. The light changed, and I moved on. The guy wasn't a threat after all; he was doing what he felt compelled to do, but he certainly had no intention of pouncing on me.

Unless someone is aiming his or her attitude, words, or body right at you, your annoyance is your choice. There are strange, annoying people everywhere, not just on the subway. There's no point in being smug about other people's behavior. For all we know, there are a lot of people who find us to be strange or annoying.

We can choose to be upset because we believe someone annoyed or wronged us, or we can lighten up and move on. In other words, don't let situations or other people define your subway ride. It's your day. It's your life.

However you respond to people who annoy you, recognize that it's only a moment in time that they actually have your attention. Get on with what you were doing, and know with certainty that somewhere down the tracks you will run into another person who will bother you.

Simplify your life. Let it go, and keep going.

O n the subway, there will be times when you need to go crosstown in order to go uptown, and that requires a transfer from one train to another. People do it all the time, sometimes every day.

In life, transfers take the form of change—changing residences, changing partners, or changing paint colors, cars, or jobs. Change is a constant fact of life.

A previous chapter (**Expect to Get Bounced Around**) focused on your emotional response to things; this chapter is about your physical response. The action you take or don't take will determine whether you successfully arrive at your destination and accomplish what you have set out to do.

An interesting coincidence in our life-as-a-subway-ride analogy is that the word *commute*, from its Latin root, means change. Change is everywhere. Life is constantly changing, and we're required to respond to it whether we really want to or not. Some people fear change. They will often make an extra effort, even if it means walking or driving twice as far to avoid having to do something different.

Granted, changing trains is not the same as changing jobs—but the one step they both require is acceptance, if you're ever going to successfully contend with change. If you choose not to change trains, you will end up at a destination you didn't really intend. The same is true in life. If you choose not to change jobs, for example, you may stay stuck in a position that will eventually become obsolete.

A transfer, or change, also means that extra effort will be called for to accomplish what you want to achieve.

Change doesn't just happen. Effort is required.

We sometimes fear change because it disrupts our comfortable pattern. But despite our best attempts at keeping things under control and predictable, breakdowns occur, trains get rerouted, and life happens.

Most of the time, change can be predicted, so it's best to be prepared and expect change as a fact of life, rather than be surprised by it. Change is a normal, expected part of life, like a subway transfer. It's neither good nor bad, it just is.

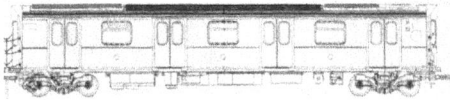

V | AWARENESS AND INTENTION

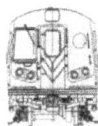

On the subway, getting off at the right stop is a matter of paying attention. All it takes is a few moments of daydreaming and suddenly you realize that you've missed your stop.

In life, getting off at the right stop can also mean recognizing when it's time to end things—jobs, relationships, trips, visits, conversations, eating, exercising, worrying ... In fact, practically everything we do in life has an end point, and an ending is usually something that is initiated by us, by someone else, or by natural causes.

Timing is everything, as they say. So before you approach your intended exit, make sure you know where you're going next and why. It's only natural. Obviously, if you're in a situation that is unhealthy or unsafe, you skip those steps and get out, but for 99% of your life, plan a destination or an end point in advance, and be on the lookout for its arrival.

Generally speaking, life is a process; there is a beginning, middle, and an end to practically everything. The problem is that many people get on board this train called life, and go for the ride with no plan. They roll along with no idea what to do next, where to go next, and with whom.

Don't misunderstand. There's nothing wrong with being a free spirit in life. It's your choice. But if you have a family, people in the community, or people at work who depend on you—then being a drifter is selfish and hurtful. On the other end of the spectrum, obsessively planning isn't the best way to live, either.

Have you ever put a pot of water on the stove to boil and forgotten about it because you became preoccupied with something? Or have you ever been driving on the interstate and zipped right past your desired exit? These are examples of inattention. Because your actions did not have serious implications attached, you probably let yourself off the hook. This is a natural response. But this response won't serve you well if you're inattention has a more serious consequence.

Just like on the subway, the way you end things successfully is by staying aware.

The clues are usually there—important decisions, life-changing choices, or relationship-ending events.

The clues are all there for you to see. How will you respond? Do you end it or keep going? It's your choice.

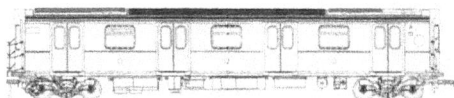

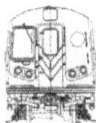

There will be times when you stop paying attention to what you are doing. Or you stop noticing your surroundings. You are no longer *positionally aware*, as pilots say. And suddenly you look up and find yourself on a deserted subway platform with a few unsavory characters eyeing you.

As much as the safety of the subway has improved, it's not the place to be at 3:30 in the morning by yourself.

Knowing the time is just another way of paying attention.

Awareness is an important part of life; it means being consistently aware of the time, the location, and the conditions around you.

Awareness doesn't require hypersensitivity. Awareness is a consistently balanced state of being, akin to checking your rearview mirror occasionally while you're driving, instead of focusing only on what's in front of you.

One of the greatest gifts you can give your children is the gift of awareness. Teach them how to be aware. Do they know what time it is? Are they aware of the conditions around them? These are lessons that will stay with them for a lifetime.

Awareness only takes a moment, no matter how busy you think you are. Whether it's a brief glance both ways before crossing the street or taking a quick accounting of a new environment you've just entered—a city, an office building, an airplane, or a subway— you're giving yourself a huge advantage.

It takes only a moment to recognize whether everything seems okay. Or to sense that there is a glaring potential problem ahead.

Maintaining awareness of the time and of your surroundings does not imply that you need to live in fear. But do take note of the time if you're going to places that are less than safe at certain hours of the day. If it's 3:30 in the morning and you're by yourself, take a cab.

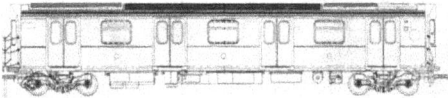

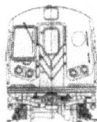

Fool them all. Make passersby wonder why you're smiling. Do the same with the rest of your life. Smile often. But make sure the smile is genuine; don't lie about how you feel. Smile with the intention to inspire others to do the same.

Happiness, like smiling, is a choice.

Not everyone believes this, but I do. Consciously look for those people and things that you genuinely like or are attracted to. This is not the same as wearing rose-colored glasses; it is, once again, about raising your awareness level concerning the people and things you really enjoy versus looking for those things that can bring you down.

Smiling is contagious. Try it with anyone you meet, a stranger or a friend. Look them right in the eye and smile. Even on the subway. Don't say a word, just smile.

If they don't smile back, I'll buy you coffee.

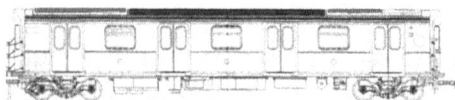

THE END OF THE RIDE
IS JUST
THE BEGINNING

The subway can be a revealing portrait of life for all of us. It can help you better understand your own life, and why you respond to people the way you do.

Despite the hundreds and thousands of people around you during your journey, many choose to be alone. They isolate with books, magazines, tablets and iPods, but that doesn't stop life from going on around them.

The subway is a mode of transportation, but it's also a place that is full of life. It can be vibrant, chaotic, and disruptive all in the same moment. You can't get much more alive than that.

The next time you're being taken for a ride— literally, on a subway, bus, taxi, or airplane—

take notice of the people around you who are busy living their lives, doing the best they can, interacting with those around them (or trying not to). Hopefully they're smiling (maybe they're frowning.) Hopefully they're energized. (Or they may be yawning.) They may be aware of their surroundings. (Or they may be completely lost—geographically and mentally.)

Then look at yourself. Not in a self-conscious way, but with the intent of self-awareness.

Are you fully engaged in your life and the life that goes on around you?

Real awareness in life is about other people—and how you respond to them. The only way you can effectively respond to people is by staying aware.

Are you aware of how you feel as you read these words?

Take a moment to notice. How do you really feel? It's not always easy to determine.

Here is a quick way to force awareness—just let go. Suppose you are traveling on a noisy, crowded, shuddering subway car. Right now, this moment, can be a perfect time to practice getting centered. Ask yourself, "What am I feeling right now?" Then answer the question, quickly, without judgment.

You've just centered yourself amidst a sea of noise. For that one split second or two, you turned your attention away from everything else and turned inward.

When you are centered, it becomes easier to deal with the noise of the world that's all around you, whether you're seated on a crowded subway car or standing on the corner of a busy intersection.

How you view your life is your choice.

You can see the subway as a new experience every day, or view it with fear and caution. (You can live your life that way, too.)

You can view the subway as a stimulating experience or simply a place to hide for a while. (You can live your life that way, too.)

Hopefully your life (and your travels) don't seem foreboding to you. Your ride through life is an opportunity to live with an expectation of happiness, to become more aware, and to become more human.

Choose to confidently ride the subway and **live your life with your eyes wide open**. Be willing to take yourself on a journey of discovery, whether you're going across town or across the country.

It's your choice whether to enjoy the ride.

Every day.

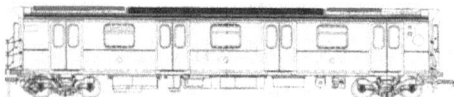

ASSESSMENT
AND
REVIEW

ASSESSMENT AND REVIEW

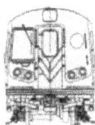

*A*t the end of a journey, it's always good to reflect on what you have experienced. What you learned and how you felt about the experience are both good questions to ask yourself. The self-assessment below is provided as a quick review of what you've just read. You may also use it as a scorecard for yourself every few months to help you refocus on what you feel is important.

CIRCUMSTANCES AND DECISIONS

- How do you deal with circumstances that come up? Are your decisions influencing what's happening?

- I am thoughtful with most decisions I make; I try hard not to make thoughtless choices because I'm busy or unfocused.

- I am able to stay focused on myself and what I want to accomplish; I've learned how to not let myself become overly distracted by the noise of the outside world.

- Decisions don't intimidate me—even the big ones. I recognize that the majority of the time, if I take a moment to think, I will make the right decision.

- I recognize and accept that life isn't always fair. I understand that there are some people who will occasionally take advantage of the system through cheating and deception.

- Although I don't like waiting, I know how to take a virtual time out whenever I feel my impatience brewing.

NAVIGATING THROUGH LIFE - *Life can sometimes feel like a maze without a map. How do you get around?*

- I am comfortable with the fact that life is an endless series of choices, and that these choices define who I am and who I will become.

- I try to embrace an abundance mentality versus one of scarcity; I don't instinctively fight for things because I believe the pie of life is a big one and there is plenty for everyone.

- Although I can be as selfish as the next person, especially when I'm bone tired, I will give up my seat or my space if I recognize that someone else may need it more than I do.

- I don't fear being roughed up by life; problems occur in everyone's life, and it's how I respond to them that makes the difference.

- For the really big decisions in life, I research and seek the counsel of people I trust. I don't make big decisions in a vacuum.

RELATING - *How do you connect with and relate to those around you?*

- Because it is easy to tune out the people around me, even family and friends, I actively push myself to stay connected.

- I smile at other people because I enjoy doing so.

- I know how to share the basic things in life with other people, even strangers, without feeling overly possessive.

- I help others or I'm kind to people because I want to be kind, not because I want praise or recognition.

- I realize that the most important thing that I can give is my time.

RESPONDING - *Things happen. You respond. How's that working?*

- I am fully aware of what is going on around me. When I'm out in public, I don't usually get lost in a daydreaming fog or in a cell phone conversation.

- I do not fear other people because I think they are looking at me strangely, but I do raise my awareness level.

- Although I don't always succeed, I have learned how to tune out or avoid people who annoy or irritate me.

- I accept that change is a fact of life.

- I rarely whine or complain about changes I don't like; I either accept them or find a way to change my own opportunities or choices.

AWARENESS AND INTENTION - *Are you able to be aware without becoming self-conscious?*

- I recognize and actively respond to situations I know I must change or end.

- Throughout my day I consciously try to stay aware of my surroundings; I'm not looking for threats (though I know they can arise occasionally). I'm actually looking for opportunities.

- As trite as it may sound, I consistently look for things to smile about—even if it's just being able to stand up and walk.

- I try to plan most activities and projects in my life—not because I'm a fanatic, but because all things have a beginning, a middle, and an end.

- I am usually consciously aware of these three things throughout my day:
    1. What I am doing
    2. How I am feeling
    3. What I am planning to do next

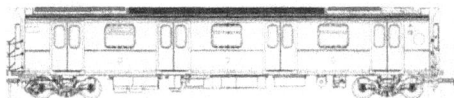

ACKNOWLEDGEMENTS

ACKNOWLEDGEMENTS

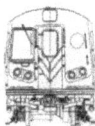

This book began as a random idea that floated from my head to paper, and then to friends and family for feedback.

My thanks to Tom and Nancy Seamon, Herb Ammons, Monte Lambert, Nick Bowers, Ann Bowers, Lauren Pasquale, Greg Behl, Cal Miller, Steve Shannon, Matt Peace, Howard Katz, and Nick Tamposi for their friendship, feedback, and guidance.

Additional thanks and acknowledgement to my brothers and sisters – Linda, Ricky, Lauren, and Jerry; and to my mother, Mary Ellen – all New Yorkers no matter where they live.

Special thanks to Sebastian, my book designer, who consistently performs great work; and the seven hour time zone difference makes it even more interesting.

Special thanks, as well, to Kammy Wood, my editor. She always makes my words sound better the second time around.

More thanks to my daughter, Vanessa, for her assistance (once more) with designing the cover. She now knows what it means to be a New Yorker having recently moved there.

Thanks, gratitude, and love to my wife, Maura, who remained patient while I pecked away at the keyboard.

Lastly…the subway really isn't as scary as it looks…and neither is life!

"Don't take any shit from anybody!"
– Billy Joel

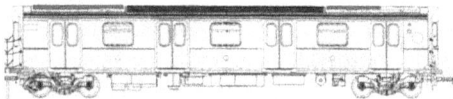

**Life is like riding the subway
without holding on.**

Jeff Pasquale is an Executive and Life Coach who works specifically in the areas of Balance, Leadership, and Teamwork. He is the author of *Looking for SUNSHINE — A Practical Guide for Dealing with Life's Challenges*, *Get That New Job*, and *Coaching Leadership – If Not You, Who?*

He lives in Boynton Beach, Florida.

More information about Jeff can be found at **www.JeffPasquale.com**

Additional tools can be found at **www.SubwayLifeTheBook.com**